LIFE AFTER 'I DO!'

LIFE AFTER 'I DO!'

Awakening from my dreams…
Learning to love the reality of
marriage and family

82196 – June 2004

Rachel Egan

3 5944 00082 1965

To order additional copies of this book, contact:
Xlibris Corporation
1-888-795-4274
www.Xlibris.com
Orders@Xlibris.com
23564

For Jay

ACKNOWLEDGMENTS

With eternal gratitude and love, special thanks to:

Editor
Rebecca Kenary

Illustrator
Lynne Kowaleski Holmes

CONTENTS

CHAPTER ONE

INTRODUCTION

"Among those whom I like or admire
I can find no common denominator,
but among those whom I love,
I can;
all of them make me laugh."

W.H. Auden

I clearly remember being furious with my mother for not understanding what I was feeling as a teenager. I swore I would never treat my kids that way when they were upset. Well, you know what? I do. My kids are adolescents and I find their hysterics and mood swings annoying, draining and hurtful. When they say, "Don't you remember what it felt like when you were my age?" I say, "Not really, so knock it off."

Well, I do want to remember what it felt like early in my marriage: becoming a couple, becoming an in-law, having children, choosing a life style and struggling with all of it. I don't know anything I was less prepared for than being married and having children, which is amazing given I can't think of anything more important in life. I had no idea the lows would be so low, the highs so high or how much I would need to learn in order to survive and enjoy it all. I thought I had finished my education; little did I know it was just beginning.

This book touches on those aspects of my life over the past eighteen years. I in no way intend this to be preachy or pretend to be an expert in any of these areas. I just know I find it comforting knowing others are going through or feeling similar things. I want to share some insights I've learned through my own experiences as a daughter, wife, in-law and mother so you can bear it in mind if some of these things happen to you. I also want to pass on wisdom I've gained by talking, listening and laughing with others who've been there, too. We get it. I hope you will be able to relate to my somewhat ordinary, but in other ways extraordinary, life.

So what gives me the expertise to write something like this? I have not won any big awards, my kids are not "gifted" and I have never run for elective office other than my parish council. To be perfectly honest, I am an average person in almost every sense. But even average people have some unique gift or talent.

Well, my mother always told me I was loaded with common sense.

I never thought of this as a compliment. But the longer I live, the more I realize what a gift common sense can be. It just helps sift through all the nonsense. It is particularly helpful when it comes to marriage and children and everything that comes with them. Although family and friends seeking me out for advice does not go over well on a resumé, it is a gift just the same . . .

rke

FINAL THOUGHT

*"Honor the talent you have been given,
otherwise it will be taken from you.
It is wise to honor at once the giver,
the gift and yourself,
to whom the gift has been given."*

Maya Angelou

CHAPTER TWO

MARRIAGE

"I can't marry Herbie, Mom," a daugther said,
"He's an atheist and doesn't believe in hell."
Her mother replied, "You marry him, and we'll show him!"

Let me preface all my marriage remarks by the fact that I married a very good guy—a real gentleman. Most days I know this, even if I don't believe it. I can usually reach that place deep inside me that knows he is not intentionally trying to destroy all my dreams of what I thought my marriage would be like. On very good days, I can actually see my part in our somewhat dull and predictable marriage. And this is where the beauty of common sense comes in. I am smart enough to know my marriage must be quite typical for most couples who have been married for a while and have kids. The grind gets to most of us. The day in and day out grunt work wears us down. I have actually gotten through some pretty low moments in my marriage because I know this is true.

Good Years / Bad Years

Riding in a limo with my father on the way to the church to be married, my father said to me, "Just remember, honey, there will be good years and bad years." Nervously laughing, I replied, "You mean good days and bad days, right?" "No," he said, "that's not what I mean."

After that little bombshell, we neared the church where I panicked and said, "I can't go in there. Can we please go for a ride?" My bridesmaids watched as our limo pulled up to the church and then quickly pulled away. My father's timing was terrible. I think at that moment the reality of marriage hit me. No wonder my father had kept saying over the last few months, "A wedding is a day, but marriage is for a lifetime . . . focus on the marriage, not the wedding." We took a ride while I did a lot of deep breathing and eventually headed back to the church.

Eighteen married years later, I understand the wisdom of my father's ill-timed words. They actually helped me through a difficult year or two. Not bad for eighteen years! Having had a bad year with Jay, I now know what my father meant. I'm so glad he prepared me because I didn't give up. Although I didn't like it, I understood it to be part of sharing my life with someone. A year is a long time to be unhappy, but before I was married I had a bad year here and there—I just didn't have a spouse to blame it on.

The "W" Theory

Years ago, a friend told me about the "W" theory as it relates to marriage. She heard it from someone who heard it from someone . . . so this is not scientifically based, but it does make sense. The theory is all marriages have natural ups and downs and they follow the pattern of the letter "W".

After the wedding, your marriage is at the top left of the "W" because everything seems wonderful, idyllic and hopeful. As the years pass, the first downward slope of the "W" begins in your marriage. The reality of living with another person, splitting chores, dealing with in-laws, the excitement and anxiety of pregnancy or not getting pregnant, and career pressures all take root. You reach the bottom of that first slope when your children are infants and toddlers. Lack of sleep, no time to yourself, lousy sex, and parental anxiety about everything from babies walking on time to those terrible immunization shots, makes you wonder . . .

Why did I get married?
Who is this guy anyway?

And no matter what your husband does, believe me, it will never be enough during this stage. Life has just gotten too big and we're too tired, and for some reason it is easier to blame your husband and marriage rather than recognizing it as a stressful time which will pass.

The slope of the "W" starts upward again when there are no more infants and toddlers. I truly believe the ages of four to eleven are magical. When your kids are in this age-range, life seems manageable again. You are still insulated from the outside world. You, as parents, hold all the answers for your kids or enough of them that you feel competent. Your kids still adore you and want to go places with you. They are becoming independent, but drugs, sex and all the other teen issues are not yet a threat. You are cruising along; your life seems pretty good and your mate pretty wonderful.

And then: adolescence strikes. Following the "**W**" path, your marriage takes a second downward turn. Once again, the marriage is tested. Intentionally or not, kids this age can and will tear you apart if you do not acknowledge adolescence for all it is. It's the time for our kids to break away from us and make us good and miserable in the process.

As an added pressure, most of us reach mid-life at this stage which brings on a whole host of our own issues. This is when it is most critical to hang in there. Take heart: the kids will be leaving soon and the marriage slope heads up again following the final right leg of the "**W**." When the kids are gone, it is clear sailing for your marriage as the "**W**" settles on its final comfortable plateau.

That's the theory anyway!

GETTING
THROUGH
DIFFICULT
TIMES . . .

Try to Listen

The biggest mistake I made in the beginning of our marriage was thinking this was the way it was always going to be. I think it takes a while to understand the huge commitment you have made to another human being. As it starts to sink in, I think both partners can become territorial and begin to fight a lot. You stop listening to each other. It can feel like a constant power struggle. Jay used to say my favorite saying was "This isn't working." I can remember getting very discouraged those first few years. I would think, "If it's not great now, won't it just get worse?" But as time goes on, if you're willing to literally shut up and listen— which I could have sworn I was doing but wasn't—things begin to change.

I did not realize I needed to become a better listener until an incident occurred while I was driving in the car with my four-year-old son, Jim. It occurred during the 1991 Persian Gulf War; we were driving in the car when a loud plane roared above us.

I said, "Wow, Jim, look at that jet!"

"Where is it going?" he asked.

"Probably California," I said.

"Mom, why is he shooting at California?"

"Who?" I asked, confused.

"The bad guy," he answered.

"What bad guy are you talking about, honey?"

"The one shooting bullets at California," he said.

"No one is shooting bullets at California," I said somewhat impatiently. "That was a plane. A jet is a plane."

"But," he said anxiously, "we're at war, right?"

I almost veered off the road. My husband and I had not discussed the war with our children. We *ASSUMED* four-year-olds worried about who gets the prize in the cereal box. Suddenly, I found myself talking about a very delicate issue. When I realized my son felt deeply threatened and was seeking reassurance from me, I changed from a passive to an engaged listener. He had many questions about the war: What is war? What is the bad guy's name? Will he hurt our house? Will he come in my room? Is he a daddy? Do his children cheer for him?

I found myself listening in a fiercely aggressive way. Also, my responses to his questions were the most thoughtful and precise I had had in years. I thought about what I wanted to say, what I needed to say, and the best way to say it. The reason I relate this story is because it was a very powerful moment which taught me the inherent risks of poor listening, thoughtless responses and the dangers of assuming. I learned I am not only accountable for what I say, but also for what I do not hear because of poor listening.

Luckily, this incident occurred early in our marriage so it helped me be open to the possibility that perhaps I was not really listening to my husband. Perhaps I had been listening selectively, to defend myself or to pick flaws in his arguments. Perhaps I needed to listen to learn about myself as my husband saw me, not just wait for my turn to speak.

Change What You Can Control

We had been married for about five years when I had a real breakthrough in my relationship with my husband. Each night, I would make a big family dinner and wait for Jay to get home from work so we could eat as "one big happy family." (Did I mention I had four children, each born a year apart?) Anyway, my husband worked very long hours. Most nights, he would *not* make it home for dinner, but more infuriating, he would not call to say he would be late or wouldn't be coming home for dinner at all. Can you imagine what a pleasant time followed when he finally did come home?

One night, I was complaining *again* to a friend of mine who had been married for quite some time. Exasperated, Janet finally said to me, "You don't get it. He's not coming home for dinner and he's not calling. Evidently, you are going to have to fight with your husband for fifteen years like I did with mine." "Oh, my God," I thought, "she's right! He's not coming home for dinner and we've already been fighting about this for five years. I don't want to fight about it for another ten years."

That very night, I fed the kids macaroni and cheese very early. I fixed myself dinner after they ate and then put the kids to bed. When Jay came in expecting dinner and a fight, he got neither.

After that night, I completely changed my routine. I pulled myself out of that victim mode and improved my life. We would not be having the family dinner I envisioned and had thought was so important, but the reality was fighting over it was destroying our marriage. I also realized his relationship with our kids was up to him.

Who knows why Jay didn't call . . . it's really not the point. The point is he didn't. To have the same fight over and over and over is crazy and exhausting. It made me miserable and negatively affected my relationship with our children.

Think Long - Term

I once asked a co-worker who had divorced and remarried, "So how is it the second time around?" expecting her to say, "Oh, he's perfect and everything is absolutely wonderful!" But instead she said, "The first time I married for love, the second time I married for love, the third time, I'm going for the gold!" This was a perfect illustration to me that there is no perfect mate or perfect marriage, no matter how much we want to believe it. A marriage is hard work, particularly if you are in it for the long term. I am not advocating staying with someone who is abusive or destructive in any way. I am talking about working through the day-in and day-out struggles of living with another human being.

Early in our marriage, Jay and I promised each other we would never mention divorce as an option to solve our problems, hoping it would make us work harder to search for other solutions. Over the years, I've adopted the attitude of doing what I need to do to be happy in my marriage and move it forward. I decided my marriage needed the same willingness and determination to succeed I would be willing to give to a job. I talk to people who I think have good marriages; I talk with my brother to get a male perspective; I read articles and books on relationships; and we've attended couples' retreats and seminars.

Recently, my husband decided to leave his job after seventeen years and start his own company. He earned a good salary with benefits and security. All of a sudden, there would be no steady income and no benefits, and did I mention our four children are all adolescents now?

Based on the "W" theory, our marriage must be feeling some pain and believe me, it is. This is a stressful time for us, like when we had infants and toddlers and he wasn't coming home for dinner. I can look back now to those earlier years and understand why it was so difficult, but when you are in something, it is very hard to get perspective. It just seems awful and endless. Recognizing this stage of our marriage for what it is (a difficult time) brings me comfort because I do believe it will pass. One thing I know for sure: when all of this uncertainty settles down, and it will, I still want to be married to Jay.

Summary

The joke is on us: marriage is really not like the movies! There are incredible tender and magical moments. There are incredible lonely and hurtful moments. Everything else is somewhere in between.

When Jay and I are going through a rough patch and are out of sorts with each other, I sometimes wonder if my marriage is worth all this effort. Especially since I feel like I'm the one who always has to change to move things forward. (My husband says he feels the same way.) But I don't let these doubts get hold of me. I believe it is all part of becoming a couple. It is a process that takes time. Once you get the hang of it, marriage can be quite wonderful.

I once heard marriages end in a whimper, which is why I firmly believe a marriage is worth fighting for. By fighting I don't mean screaming and shouting, but rather trying different things until it feels right for both of you. There's a lot of wisdom in the old adage "everybody is half right." Did I sell out by giving up on my husband coming home for dinner or at least calling? Maybe. But coming to terms with winning a few and losing a few can go a long way. I created a new life-style for myself and my children at the dinner hour that I actually enjoyed. We also started having breakfast as a family, which worked out fabulously since my kids always seemed to wake up at 6:00 A.M.! I had to let go of what I thought my marriage should be and embrace it for the reality it was.

In 1588, Montaigne said, "Marriage may be compared to a cage: the birds outside frantic to get in and those inside frantic to get out." In my marriage today, patience plays as big a role as passion; listening actually leads to lust; and sharing a complex history together is an intimacy all its own.

One day I asked my father if he thought I had a good marriage. He said, "If you want to go somewhere, does Jay want to go with you?"

"Yes . . ." I answered.

"If Jay wanted you to go with him, like to Maine for the day, would you want to go with him?"

"Most times," I replied.

"Well, then," he said, "that's good."

For some reason, his answer just made me laugh. What he said was so simple but so true!

Techniques

Stop and Observe Your Fights . . .

It takes two to fight, but one to stop a fight. If you are fighting about the same thing over and over and over—stop it. Wave the white flag and say, "You win!" In a marriage, someone always feels as though they are losing. Realize that losing a battle isn't so bad because many, many fights are just stupid and territorial. If losing allows you to move on . . . become a happy loser! As in all sports, there is nothing more moving than a gracious loser. Besides, if you learn something about yourself and your relationship, then you haven't really lost. Come to terms with irresolvable problems.

Bring Down the Glass Dome . . .

When I am trying to change my behavior and not fight with my husband, I pretend a glass dome is descending around me. When the dome is down, I can't hear what my husband is saying and he can't hear me, so it is pointless to say anything (I got this one from an old TV show "Get Smart"). Sometimes I need to play games with myself to get through difficult moments. I can get stuck in one way of seeing, feeling and re-acting to my husband because he knows how to push my buttons and make me truly neurotic. The trick is to change this pattern and the make-pretend glass dome really helps me do this.

(Hint: It also works well with adolescents!)

Keep a Journal . . .

I write down the things I whisper to myself as I walk away from a fight. Whispers are very revealing—listen to them, write them down. Writing in my journal helps me not say things I might later regret. By writing it down and reading it when I have calmed down, it usually becomes apparent to me I am blaming everyone, everything and everyplace except myself when I am feeling overwhelmed with life. It helps me see my part in things and helps me recognize it might just be me who needs to do some adjusting. It reinforces the key concept that I really only have control over myself.

Pull a Scarlet O'Hara—"I'll just worry about that tomorrow" . . .

Things do not always have to be dealt with immediately. Some things are better left alone for a while . . . not forever, just a while. When we are in a particularly bad place and I know our fighting could go nuclear, I will make a conscious decision not to worry or have a breakdown until a certain date. For example, when my husband was starting his business, rather than get hysterical, critical and nag him daily, I promised myself I would try to keep my mouth shut for three months and *then* allow myself to have a meltdown.

Another example of the Scarlet style would be, as I heard someone say recently, "The day my youngest child goes out the front door to college, I'm leaving out the back."

This thought may be enough to get you through "the moment," which is all we're trying to do. If the "W theory" holds, when your kids leave for college your marriage will be in a much better place. You will actually like each other again and not want to leave at all.

Try Not to Nag . . .

When I first dated my husband, I smoked cigarettes. He never complained about my smoking. One day when I was puffing away I said, "I can't believe it doesn't bother you that I smoke." He said, "Of course it bothers me. I hate it." I always assumed if something bothers you, you nag and badger . . . Well, Jay never said another word about it, but I became more and more uncomfortable smoking around him and finally gave it up. I think if he had nagged me to stop I would still be smoking today.

Become a Cheerleader . . .

One day my friend, Lynne, told me I encouraged her to be her husband's cheerleader. I said, "You have got to be kidding. Did I really say that?" She said I had and it changed the way she related to her husband. "I had fallen into a habit of nagging my husband and focusing on the negative rather than the positive. Your comment made me remember we were on the same team."

I told my husband what Lynne had said and he just started laughing. He reminded me of my behavior a few days earlier. I had been irritated with him for some reason but I kept following him around. He finally asked me why I continued to trail him around when it was so clear he was aggravating me. My response was, "Here's the deal: I like you even when you're an asshole!"

How's that for cheerleading? I'm not proud of the last line, but let's face it, some days are better than others.

FINAL THOUGHT

I asked my Grandmother Kenary
why she thought she had such a good marriage.
She said,
"We always blamed ourselves
rather than each other."

Note(s) to Self...

CHAPTER THREE

In-laws

"My mother in-law just got back from Kabul.
She was teaching the Taliban how to fight dirty."

*Jim Kenary**

My granddaughter came to me and asked,
"When are we going to play football?"
I told her little girls don't play football.
So she asked me why her mother had said,
"When Grandpa kicks off, we're going to be rich!"

Jim Kenary

---

*   Jim Kenary is my father. He says these are his jokes. Even if he heard them somewhere else, he's told them *so many times* I think he deserves credit!

When Jay and I told his mother we were engaged she started crying and asked us not to tell his sisters; she would break the news to them herself. This probably should have clued me into a few things, but to be honest it confused me. I was young, naive and in love, so I *assumed* those were tears of joy. I thought she wanted to be the one to spread the good news. Did I mention my husband is the only boy in a family with three older sisters?

A New Family is Born

I'm not brave enough to write a lot about this subject because it is too loaded with land mines. I could tell you some incredible stories about my in-laws, but I'm sure Jay has a few of his own to share about my family, so we'll just leave it at that. If you're blessed with the perfect family and in-laws, cherish it. For most of us, there are issues! There are issues about holidays or naming a baby or calling this one and not inviting that one or a sick parent or a dysfunctional sibling or spending more time with "his" people or . . . . whatever.

Dr. Carl A. Whitaker, a pioneer of family therapy, has said "Marriage is a battle between two families struggling to reproduce themselves." This would explain why, when my son was born, my mother looked at him and said, "Oh, he's not a Kenary." Not "Doesn't he look just like an Egan!"

In-laws can be a source of great comfort, but it was the great distress they can and do cause that surprised me. You think, I love my mate and they love my mate, so aren't we all on the same team? It's a tough realization when you learn not only are you not on the same team, but if you don't play by certain rules- which you didn't even know existed—you are out! I know Jay feels as deeply about his family as I feel about mine. So if someone in his family is causing a problem and it is hurting us and affecting our marriage, I try to believe it is hurting him more than it is hurting me.

As adults, we need to come to terms with our families. You can't deny they exist nor would you want to because they are part of your very fiber. We still need our families, but in a new way. It is crucial to put our new family first. The sooner you realize that you and your mate are a *new family*, the better off your marriage will be. Rather than "my people" are right or "his people" are wrong, try to believe everyone is half right and take it from there. The fact is you are not going to change his family and he is not going to change yours—these dynamics have been in place for a long, long time. They are intricate, complicated and indestructible.

As a couple, you need to come up with your own ways of doing things and your own traditions. Running around doing what is best for his family or your family is a huge waste of time because you can't possibly please everyone. But you can please each other! Make your marriage your first priority. See yourselves as a new family. You have power and control over your *new family* and that is it. Don't give that power away! Bring the glass dome down around the two of you when outside forces try to convince you otherwise. It is important to focus on each other and set new boundaries. If you don't, either his family or your family will set the boundaries for you.

Learn to Say NO

Learning to say "No" to our families and "Yes" to each other did not come naturally for Jay and me. And we paid a price. As I mentioned, if you don't set up boundaries as a couple, someone else will set them for you. We eventually learned to prioritize each other, but in the meantime there was a lot of hurt that could have been avoided if we had not felt so guilty saying "No." I don't know why it was easier to hurt each other, but it was.

Learning to say "No" is a skill I am still trying to develop. I did not even realize it was a skill until I read an incredible book on the subject: *When I Say No, I Feel Guilty* by Dr. Manuel J. Smith. It changed my life. My older brother has been a great role model in this respect. He learned how to say no from a roommate in college. His roommate never gave excuses when asked to do something he did not want to do; he would just say "No." My father also provided inspiration with this quote from a friend, "If someone has the nerve to ask, you should have the nerve to say No."

After reading about saying "No," talking about saying "No" and practicing saying "No," I am finally getting better at it. The kids' school called recently and asked me to be on a committee. I said, "Thank you so much for thinking of me, but No." It was a giddy almost powerful feeling. I didn't gush and go on about the other committees I was on or how busy I was—I just said, "Thank you, No." If I had said yes to that committee, I would have been furious with myself when I hung up the phone and angry every time I went to a meeting. I have enough anger in my life; I would rather feel momentary guilt (but relief) than recurring anger and frustration.

Be Forgiving/Apologize

Family members (this includes in-laws) can hurt us on a level we never expected or could have imagined. When this happens, the situation can become complicated and messy because of the depths of our feelings. And you can't just hide or disappear until the hurt goes away. It is almost impossible to cut a family member off from your life and not suffer for it for as long as the standoff continues.

It's easy to forgive minor infractions, but otherwise forgiveness is tough and so is apologizing. When it comes to family and in-laws, as in a marriage, there are irresolvable problems. People say and do things they shouldn't and people get hurt . . . really hurt. When certain emotions get hold of you—rage, hate, jealousy—and they are caused by your own family or in-laws, it will deeply affect your marriage even though your spouse is not causing the problem. These situations need to be dealt with. You need to protect your new family. You need to move on. To do this, you need to open your heart to forgiveness and even be willing to apologize.

I still remember the first time my mother apologized to me . . . I don't remember what had caused the problem but I can still feel how special the moment was for us. It was very powerful and, in some ways, a transforming experience. It helped me remember my mom is just a person doing the best she can and, like the rest of us, making some mistakes along the way. It taught me about my own readiness and willingness to forgive, but even more important it taught me the power of an apology.

In our conversation that day, she told me her own mother had never apologized to her. She also told me she was surprised by how good it felt. It felt good to me, too, and I know this experience has helped me be able to apologize to my own children.

Learning to forgive or offer an apology is just as much a skill as learning to say "No." For most of us, it does not come naturally. To become a forgiving person takes practice, especially when the hurt is brought on by those we love or the people/family they love. There are always lessons to be learned from painful experiences. For me, the scars they leave remind me of my vulnerability but also of my heart's ability to heal when I am willing to forgive.

One time a priest explained forgiveness to me in a way that made it seem easier to do. He said, "When someone hurts you intentionally or has caused you a great injustice and you decide to forgive them, it does not mean you will feel the same way towards that person. Nor does it mean it is up to you to make the relationship right again. Your relationship will never be the way it was before, but it is important not to retaliate and sink down to that person's level. Forgiveness is trying to stay kind towards that person so they can come back up to your level." Being kind to people who have hurt me is not always easy, but it seems easier now that I see it as an act of forgiveness.

Summary

A few years ago, we went to visit my parents at the beach. Jay and I were fighting about something; I honestly cannot remember what it was about, but it seemed monumental at the time. Anyway, usually when we are angry with each other, no one would ever know. We really try not to let others in on our differences. This time though, I just could not fake it. I was so mad I couldn't talk to him or even hide my anger. It was quite uncomfortable for my parents. My father, who prefers "peace at all cost," was beside himself. He kept trying to tell me what a great guy Jay was, what a beautiful family we had, that my problems were a blessing. Ha!

I eventually stormed to the beach alone, without Jay or the kids, and was fuming away when my mother came down. I was just waiting for her to tell me to "let it go" or "be the big person" or whatever. When she approached me, my back was way up and I was ready to fight with her too. Then she said, "I don't know what you and Jay are fighting about, but whatever it is, I want you to know, I'm on your side." I burst out laughing. What she said was so perfect. It was just what I needed to hear. It completely diffused the situation because all of a sudden I was afraid for Jay!

Whether your own family or your in-laws are wonderful or hateful, they can keep you looking back and away from each other. They can cause some pretty ugly and hurtful experiences that will either tear you apart as a couple or bond you together. It is part of the process of becoming a new family. Realizing you are not one big, happy, extended family can be quite a letdown. But if you are willing to see the situation for what it is and to set boundaries which prioritize your new family, the other extended-family relationships eventually fall into place.

Helpful Hints

Dealing with hateful In-laws:	Smile, be polite and in your head repeat— "It must be awful to be you!" or . . . Smile, look bewildered and say— "Oh, that was mean. Did you say that to hurt me?"
Naming your *own* Children:	Decide with your spouse.
Where to go for the Holidays:	Decide with your spouse.
Most things:	Decide with your spouse.
Most other things:	Pretend you decide with your spouse!
Try to Believe:	If someone in your spouse's family is causing a problem and it is hurting you and your marriage, it is hurting your spouse more.
Picking future mates:	Take a good long look at the person's family . . . —it is so loaded with clues it isn't even funny!

FINAL THOUGHT

Nobody's family can hang out the sign—
"Nothing the matter here."

Chinese proverb

Note(s) to Self . . .

CHAPTER FOUR

CHILDREN

"Before I got married,
I had six theories about bringing up children.
Now, I have six children and no theories."

John Wilmot

ADJUSTING
&
SURVIVING

When my four children were all babies, people would say to me "Enjoy them now." I wanted to scream, "You have got to be kidding. They cry, they mess, they destroy things . . . They are sucking every ounce of life and self-confidence right out of me!" I didn't always feel that bad, but many days I did. If this was when I was supposed to enjoy my children most, then I was in deep trouble.

The "Keeping Up" Syndrome

Let the competitions begin!

I was never someone caught up in what other people have or do not have. I didn't understand "keeping up with the Jones" until I had kids. The emotions took me by surprise because they were really foreign to me. It began when I was pregnant with my first child. Have you signed him/her up for pre-school? There is a waiting list, you know. (A waiting list for kids to paint?!) I just could not bring myself to enroll a child who had not been born yet for anything. I felt like it was playing with the gods. I thought, shouldn't I get to know the child first?

How I eventually chose a pre-school for my child is nothing to brag about, but the reality of my life. As it turned out, the school that was so impossible to get into actually had openings when it was time for my son to go, so I went to check it out. By this time, I also had two more babies. To make a long story short, this to-die-for pre-school was on a very busy street. As I crossed the street with my children (ages two, one and three months) I thought, "I don't care how good a school this is; I am not crossing this busy street every day with all these babies."

I went to the "next best" school the following day. I had a 9:00 A.M. appointment and discovered the pre-school was on the second floor of a building with no elevator. When I reached the top of the stairs, I knew there was no way I would be climbing those stairs every day with three babies.

I then went to a religious nursery school which was not our religion and my kids would be the only ones there not of this faith. The school had a good reputation, but more importantly, it was close to my house, on a quiet street and on the ground floor. This is where I sent my son to preschool. And he loved it.

This was a defining moment for me as a mother. At the time I thought I was settling for something that was not "the best" in order to survive this period in my family's life. I was accepting "good enough" as a compromise. As the years passed, I became a huge fan of "good enough." Because you know what? "The best"—the cream of the crop, the top school, the best soccer league—never stops coming at you. I decided I wasn't playing that game anymore. I took my ball and went home.

Over time and through experience, I learned no one place or group has it all anyway. Choices are rarely best versus awful or even good versus better. They are most often good versus good. Everything in life is a trade-off. For example, if you choose a private or religious school, your children will not be exposed to the diversity of public schools; if you choose a public school, they will not experience the rituals and traditions of religious education. Who's to say which is better or more important?

With this new attitude and after a few years of morning pre-school, I decided to find an afternoon pre-school. I realized I was more of a morning person and actually liked my kids more in the morning. It was as the day wore on that my enthusiasm toward them diminished. So that is how and why I chose my next pre-school.

Sleeping

One time, I asked my mother what she thought of my kids and she said, "Well, at least they're good eaters and sleepers." I was thoroughly insulted at the time. But you know what? They *were* good eaters and sleepers and that is a start.

Early on, I read or someone told me that babies need lots of sleep because this is when their brains develop and sleeping long and well is a skill babies can learn. I also read somewhere that babies have a natural alarm clock which determines when they will wake up. So if their natural alarm is 6:00 A.M., they will wake up at 6:00 A.M. no matter when you put them to bed. So the only way to get more sleep out of babies is to put them to bed earlier.

I decided to test this theory by putting them to bed earlier and earlier, rationalizing that their brains were developing. I went from 7:00 P.M. to 6:45 P.M. to 6:30 P.M. to 6:15 P.M. to 6:00 P.M. to 5:45 P.M. . . . . The earliest I ever put them down was 4:30 P.M. and I swear they slept until 6:00 the next morning. I must have felt guilty about how much they slept because I mentioned it to my pediatrician. He told me to enjoy it because eventually they would wake up. They did; but for years they slept a good twelve hours every night.

My husband thinks I can't remember the name of the book or who told me these sleep theories because I made it up but I really don't think I did. Jay used to feel like Paul Revere back then because if the front porch light was on he could park in the driveway, but if it wasn't on he had to park down the street. It used to drive me crazy when I had just gotten all the kids settled in bed and they would hear my husband's car pull in the driveway and get all revved up for a few more hours.

One day I was in the grocery store and on the verge of tears, feeling totally exhausted and overwhelmed. I was just there to pick up a few things and hoped I wouldn't see anyone I knew. So of course I spotted a neighbor from years ago at the end of an aisle. When I was a little girl I used to wait for her to get home from work. She was always so kind and warm and usually gave me candy or gum. She is also the type of person who can just look at you and know something is wrong. I was praying she didn't see me and made a bee line to another aisle.

I was heading for the check-out and thought I was home free when I heard her say, "Honey, what's the matter?" I burst out crying and said, "Oh Martha, I don't know! I think I'm just tired . . . My kids seem out of control and I don't think I'm very good at this mother thing." She was wonderful, as usual. But what touched me most was a few days later I received a card from her. On the cover was a mother lovingly looking at her two children sleeping and she was saying, "If only I could think of them as sleeping . . ." and on the inside of the card, ". . . Instead of recharging!"

Quiet Time

Quiet time, which is what we called it, took over when naps started to end. It was the hour and a half (12:30-2:00) each afternoon when the children played alone and quietly in their rooms. Quiet time gave me the space and alone time I needed. It also helped my kids become comfortable being alone and to learn how to entertain themselves. But to be honest I would have done it regardless of this benefit; it is a long day home with kids!

Starting quiet time as naps were ending made it a very natural transition. I told the children since they no longer needed naps they were ready for the special privilege of quiet time! We kept it up for years on weekends, summers and vacations once the kids were in school.

When my grandmother, Nana, lay dying in the hospital she said to me, "I'm not worried about leaving you. Jay loves you so much; he'll take care of you, and you take care of Jim. He'll grow up to be a fine man just like his father. Always, always lead a quiet life." Upset at the time, I could not see the wisdom in her words. But I came to understand what she was trying to tell me about quiet time. When my house is quiet and still, but I can hear my kids playing contentedly in their rooms—that's good stuff. Reveling in the quiet helps me realize and be grateful for my many blessings.

Birth of the Mini-Maid

Growing up, my mother used to ask me to do a lot more chores than my siblings. I felt very resentful inside but I usually didn't show it. Actually I might sulk, but I never talked back . . . and I would do what she asked. My siblings would talk back and give her grief, so looking back I now understand it was just easier for my mother to ask me to do things.

One day I realized I was doing the same thing to one of my daughters. I was asking way more of her than the others because she wouldn't give me any guff. On the day of my revelation, Abigail stomped away when I asked her to do something. This was unlike her . . . and it made me realize, she did mind. I instantly forgave my mother for over-asking me. I understood then that she didn't do it to take advantage of me; she did it to keep things moving. I also realized I was probably a great comfort to her because she *could* ask and also because things *would* get done.

With kids, the nitpicking and bickering can be wilting. For years I struggled with how my kids could and should help me around the house. I would ask one to bring up the laundry and they would say I had just asked them and it was someone else's turn. To be honest, I couldn't remember who I had asked to do what when. We would get into an argument and very often I would end up doing the task myself. So one weekend when my husband and I were away alone together and could actually talk and think things through, we invented the mini-maid.

This is how it works for us. Since we have four children, we decided one child would be assigned to be our mini-maid for one week at a time. So besides their regular chores of keeping their rooms clean, making and changing their beds, etc., this particular child/mini-maid is at our disposal for anything and everything that week. This involves emptying wastebaskets, clearing the table, helping prepare dinner, taking out the trash . . . whatever. It has worked out amazingly well. I think the kids enjoy it, too, because it's fair and since there are four of them, it's only once a month.

A special benefit of this has been some wonderful tender moments working alongside whoever is the mini-maid. Looking back, I don't think my kids did not want to help or do their part; they just needed a system that was fair. Like the rest of us, they don't want to feel taken advantage of.

I told a friend who has five kids about our new mini-maid service. She said she would try it because she was experiencing the same frustration I had. She talked it over with her husband who said, "I don't think it will work, but let's give it a shot." When they presented the plan to their children, her oldest son wanted to know who had given them this bright idea. She told him it was the brilliant creation of an expert on family dynamics. He agreed to do whatever she wanted as long as she didn't call him a mini-maid!

Because they have five kids, they decided to assign each child one day during the week. A couple of weeks into it my friend called all excited about how well it was working for them. She said she knew it was a hit the night before when her husband had yelled, "Where's my mini-maid?"

When my sister comes over and she needs something, she'll ask, "Who's the merry-maid this week?" Whatever you want to call it or however you want to do it, it may just be worth a try.

LEARNING
ABOUT
TEMPERAMENT

I took a quiz once to determine my personality traits. The point of the quiz was to illustrate how we are all wired differently. Some people are high strung, some are easy-going, some overly-sensitive, etc. How we are wired determines how we look at and react to the world.

For example, let's say growing up my mother came into a room where I was playing with my brothers and sister and said, "This room is a mess." My older brother would think, "So?"; my sister might think, "It looks fine to me;" and my younger brother could think, "It is a mess, we should pick it up." *My* first thought would have been, "I can't believe she thinks I'm a slob." With an overly-sensitive personality, comments about a room became a personal attack.

I did not fully understand this about myself—no matter how many personality quizzes I took—until I had my own children and spotted similar traits in them. Nothing prepared me for the insights I would gain into my own personality as a result of having children. There were so many things I was unaware of . . . Childhood memories came flooding back but at a very different angle. Rather than resentment, I now felt a deep and appreciative respect for my parents and how they handled certain situations. In some ways, the memories also brought on a new self-respect. I was never trying to be super sensitive . . . that's just how I'm wired.

From the moment my children entered this world, they were each completely different. They each seemed to come with a temperament, a personality and an agenda. Jim and Emily were, for the most part, very easy babies. I was beginning to think I was a pretty good mother and then came . . . Rachel Abbott!

A Difficult Child

By the time my daughter Rachel was three, I had brought her to the pediatrician dozens of times because her behavior was so terrible. She seemed to fight and scream with everyone about everything. He asked me to tell him some good things about her and good things she did. I couldn't think of any so he had me keep a star chart. Every time I noticed her doing something good I was to put a star up on the refrigerator. He said the star chart was for my benefit; I was in such a negative cycle with this particular child that I could no longer see anything positive. Enjoy them now—hah! I am keeping a star chart to try and survive.

Looking back I think Rachel was born angry or, to be more accurate, in distress. She was colicky so she cried and screamed and cried some more. I was grateful she was our third child because we were pretty confident in our parenting skills by then, but nothing seemed to comfort her. When the colicky months passed and she became a toddler, she was still angry and difficult. Our other kids we could distract, outsmart, cajole—not this one. Sometimes I wish everyone would have a child like this so they wouldn't be so quick to give the dirty look or say, "No child of mine would be allowed to act that way." Believe me, it isn't always that simple.

With Rachel, we were constantly calling our pediatrician, Dr. John Duggan, and saying something must be wrong. He was absolutely wonderful. He would listen so patiently, check her out *again* and conclude, yes, she was difficult and had a temperamental personality. But he also insisted this did not mean something was wrong with her physically or emotionally. He said, "You don't want to put a label on her just to make yourselves feel better." He claimed as she got older and had more of her own success (away from her siblings who are so close in age), she would become less frustrated. He jokingly told us to send her to medical school when she gets older because there are so many difficult people there!

A big source of comfort and strength for me at this time was *The Difficult Child* by Dr. Stanley Turecki. Among the many important things I learned from this wonderful book was difficult children are often overly sensitive to sight, sound or touch. All of a sudden, the epic battles that I had with Rachel when I tried to brush her hair made sense. She wasn't trying to be difficult or hurtful to me, she was just trying to avoid a situation that caused her physical pain.

One time, Rachel said she wanted to take dance classes. I thought this was great because none of the other kids were interested in dancing and it could be her own thing. There was a glitch, though; she said she would not wear the black leotard dance studios required. If Rachel said she wouldn't wear something, it really meant she would not wear it. To refer again to *The Difficult Child*, Dr. Turecki claimed these kids were really not trying to be difficult in refusing to wear certain things; their skin can be so sensitive that certain materials are actually painful for them to wear.

I began calling dance studios to see if someone would allow this. The first person I called said, "Heavens, no, that would be like a football player not wearing his pads!" Oh, please! The second person I called said, "It sounds like Rachel has a problem with her self-esteem; would you like me to talk to her?" You can imagine what I wanted to answer but all I said was, "No thank you." After many calls and when I had just about given up, I called Joanne Warren Studios. Joanne herself happened to answer and I explained my plight. She said, "All the other girls will be wearing the leotards but if it doesn't bother Rachel, it doesn't bother me." Rachel took dance there for four years and loved it. She even began wearing the black leotard her third year.

Rachel adjusted to preschool beautifully; she made friends easily and did not give her teachers a hard time. At the time this amazed us. However, as our pediatrician had predicted, when she began to experience success on her own outside the family, her frustration level began to drop. She started sharing more of the engaging, funny and warm part of her personality. She also began finding her way in our family.

One day several years ago Rachel and I went skiing, just the two of us. With four children, one-on-one time is all too rare. The first couple of hours she gave me a hard time, nothing specific, just pushing all my buttons. I kept my mouth shut and just prayed for patience. All of a sudden, it was as though the demons left her. She became warm, funny and a joy to be with. I think that, being overly sensitive (like her mother), she was so excited to be skiing with just me that she had been overwhelmed by her emotions, which is when she acts out. I usually react harshly when she acts out and we get into a negative spiral. We had the best time together that day. I fell in love with Rachel all over again and it was a turning point in our relationship. The last run up the chair lift she awkwardly blurted out "I just love us!"

Today, Rachel is focused, intense and an incredibly neat kid. Believe me when I say I am only telling Rachel stories because her temperament was the most challenging for us to deal with. It was all so unexpected. But because of her, I was able to learn to see *each* of my children for who they are .

Appreciating the Differences

Each child is so unique for so many reasons such as: temperament, birth order and motivation. Having grown up in a family with four children, I experienced first-hand the effect a child's placement in the family can have on their personality. My two brothers, one the eldest of the siblings and the other the youngest, are totally different as far as personality, interests, motivation, etc. Sister Carol Skehan, who taught all of my children in kindergarten, helped me to be more aware of Jim, Emily, Rachel and Abigail's differences, particularly when it came to motivation.

Sister Carol was an absolutely wonderful teacher, so aware of and in tune with the kids. She observed that our oldest child, Jim, is motivated because he wants to please Jay and me. Our oldest daughter, Emily, tries hard because she wants to do better than everyone else in her class. Rachel is motivated from within, which, Sister Carol said, is where real passion comes from. (Her observation about Rachel fit perfectly with *The Difficult Child*.)

Our youngest daughter, Abigail, is just happy to be alive. In her written evaluation of Abigail, Sister Carol wrote, "Abigail is like a cute little honey bee busily moving from activity to activity, never causing a commotion, just focused on what has to be done. She doesn't let things/ people distract her from her mission. She plays the same as she works . . . she puts her whole self into it and doesn't get hung up on the squabbles of everyday life like the rest of us." Why can't I be wired like that?

Sister Carol's insight helped me not only to appreciate the different temperaments and motivations of my children, but to use them to their advantage. It enabled me to learn the best way to motivate each of my children to want to achieve their best.

Overlooking the Quiet One

I wrote the following poem for a writing class I took when my children were very young. I expected to learn about writing in this class . . .

My youngest girl reminds me of spring

She sings and hums like joyous birds returning home
A noticeable skip or lilt in her walk

She smells like new flowers bursting through the ground
Simply delicious

Her eyes glow
Always expecting something pleasant around the bend

Her great full lips let cries of delight and laughter roll out easily
And wash all over me

When she hugs
We melt into one
How easy it is to love this child

My middle girl also reminds me of spring

She turns green with jealousy
Like vines competing for the sun

She explodes into and onto a scene
An unexpected thunder storm

Her eyes always watch
Like the squirrel watching the new bird feeder

Her lips thin and tense
Fight with a smile trying to escape

She jabs at my heart
A rose bush with thorns

She needs more hugs
I feel my body tense
It is with this child I learned to love

When the class critiqued this poem, I was nervously expecting people not to understand my feelings, but that was not their problem with the poem at all. What concerned them was the fact I had left out my oldest daughter, Emily. Why wasn't she part of the poem? I was taken off guard. I really did not have an answer . . .

As I reflected, I realized I often paid less attention to my oldest daughter because she's very independent and self-sufficient. Quite honestly, I forget she needs me. She doesn't ask for a lot, so as in many life situations, the squeaky wheel gets my time and focus.

Emily hardly ever squeaks. I suddenly felt a hollowness in my stomach. I immediately made a conscious effort to seek Emily out more. I'm so thankful I realized this invaluable lesson when Emily was still fairly young.

Summary

Most of my theories on how to raise children pretty much went right out the window once I had them. I have done things and said things and thought things about my children I would never have imagined possible. Although there are many, many moments I gush with love and pride, the fact that I sometimes really dislike my children (or, to be kinder and gentler, dislike their behavior) is very unsettling.

One time when I was very tired and very pregnant, I was changing my daughter Emily's diaper when she wound up and kicked me as hard as she could in the stomach. I wanted so badly to strike her back. My mother happened to call and I burst out crying. Between sobs I tried to explain the rage I was feeling toward Emily. She said, "Honey, that's normal. Just stay away from her until you calm down. We've all felt that way about each of our kids at some point."

As a relatively new and naïve young mother, I was shocked my mother was not completely horrified by what I had just told her. I could not believe these feelings were normal. When my mother revealed she and many other mothers had felt the same way—I began to calm down. Maybe I was not as much of a nut case as I feared.

Over the years, raising children has taught me all about the gray area in life because there are no easy or definite answers. Each child is so different and just when you think you know what to do, a new age, stage or challenge arises.

When *stuff happens* with my kids and it always does, whether it is a health problem or a behavioral problem or whatever, I am smart enough to know when I don't know enough to make a good decision so I educate myself. I read as much on the subject as possible. I also talk to other parents—particularly those with children older than mine who have been through similar situations successfully. I have even attended seminars in areas I knew nothing about. There really are amazing resources available.

When all else fails—HUG! Sometimes a hug is what a child needs. It transfers your calm if they are out of control; it transmits your warmth and security if they are upset, and sometimes it just pulls them back from a bad place. It always amazes me how much a hug can help even when it is the last thing in the world I feel like doing. Usually once I start the hug I don't want to let go. It grounds us both.

FINAL THOUGHT

The following is one of the most beautiful gifts I ever received . . .

Merry Christmas and a Happy New Year
Mr. & Mrs. Jay Egan and Family
December 25, 1991

Not knowing how to, or what to give to you and your family as a 'gift from the heart' I came upon a 'thought' so from my 'heart to your hearts' a thought to share with all of you.

If I remember correctly, I became a sitter for you around February of 1990. A time of my life when I was experiencing and suffering from a trauma that affects all of us in different ways. Looking back to that time, I remember how much I received from the Egan children that could never be expressed here. Oh my yes, it is a lot of work, requires more patience and fortitude than you feel you have—but the naturalness, the honesty, the beauty of each individual child that you entrusted me to care for, glows from each, in their own specific, noticeable, differences.

When I began, Rachel Abbott was the youngest, just toddling around and even then, understanding, when you asked me if I would like a cup of tea during our first talk—running out to the kitchen, knowing that is where the tea is . . . Both Jim and Emily putting me to the test—The first summer we took a lot of walks together; somehow, this past summer that did not happen often because there is now the bundle of joy, Abigail.

Jim:

As I watched him go upstairs, when he came home from the Houstons the other evening—I not only saw him as a little boy—but the forming of a man with great strength and potential . . . there was a special feeling I experienced with him walking up those stairs, a feeling knowing that all is well with Jim—he struggling with his left-handedness, his understanding of being careful with his sisters—he loves a little rough and tumble from time to time, and his healthy imagination can sometimes be thwarted by competition he experiences around him—but he makes it through, and expresses himself quite well and I wished that I had written down all those wonderful things he told me about . . . his conversations about Indians, teepees, bat man, his loving family . . . in particular, "my dad", "my mom" . . . speaking small French phrases(?) . . . his genuine laughter . . . I tend to treat Jim older than his years, sometimes . . . but he appears to handle that kind of stress-well. I was the older child in my family, so I understand. I know you are proud of this little fellow! I AM.

Emily:

Now, here is a special child, and she will tell you she is a special child! Indeed, I can see her on stage—her beauty is extraordinary, inside and outside. Her imagination is wonderful. To me, she was difficult to get close to and I worked hard at that, as she always, without fail, never ceases to test me to see where I am coming from (even now) . . . I remember the hard times she gave me going to bed and . . . after trying different things . . . remember the breathing? Well, racing up the stairs is better, works better, and the genuine laughter is a joy to hear. Her stories are long and complicated, but, give her something to do—it gets done! She pretends to be rough and tough—but she really is loveable and soft, likes to cuddle, pretends not to . . . let see . . . she even talked about 'hibernation' AND she kissed me goodbye after Saturday's sitting, no one could receive a nicer gift than that from such an interesting, curious child, as my friend, Emily.

Rachel Abbott:

A sweet, sensitive, little lady that is trying not to be left out of the circle of family life; she is a survivor, strong, insistent, yet, I see gentleness behind those pretty blue eyes. I always tell all the children how nice they look, and how hard they try and do as they are told—but in particular, I express to Rachel, mostly just for her, how pretty, how capable, how well she acts, etc. and we cuddle sometimes and talk about her doll . . . One of those times I remarked to her how pretty her eyes are . . . and "Rachel, sometimes I wonder what is going on back there—in back of your pretty blue eyes" the reply, "Fiddis, my mind is back there." Needless to say, one is 'struck' when you hear that kind of reply from one so young . . . why the tears sprung to my eyes, as she laughed and smiled at me! According to Rachel sometimes, we are friends, and sometimes we are not. She is growing up!

Abigail:

I never thought that I would have the pleasure of holding a baby again. New babies are not going to happen again with my family. A new baby is special and there are a lot of repeats of some happenings from the others, as babies—but somehow, Abi is different and right from the start it was noticeable that she had something you did not see in the others. She is easy to care for, but, you have to remain alert at all times . . . All the children love her—her natural laugh is like the sound of little bells.

Jay and Rachel, you have to know that you are terrific parents and the teamwork I see—the difficulties with the children—the happiness and laughter you must experience every day with these little ones will soon be precious memories in good times and bad . . . I know that sometimes people will say—oh, you will get your reward in heaven— that may be true, but bringing up this little family in trouble times, watching them grow, hearing their laughter, tears, frustrations and conversations, experiences, illnesses wrapped up all together in beautiful silver and gold threads of life, is a reward in itself. You will, in time, know that in your heart of hearts, but you can look at each other today and say—YES, WE ARE GREAT PARENTS . . . GREAT PEOPLE ACCOMPLISH GREAT THINGS . . . and you will.

I hope you will remember me and send me an invitation to Emily's party after she receives her first Oscar! And an autographed copy of (one of many) Rachel Abbott's new book, number one on the best sellers list, an autographed picture of Jim, at the Pentagon, and Abigail, Ambassadress to France.

Merry Christmas to you and yours. Thank you for the trust and sharing in the care of your most precious children.

Warmest regards,

Phyllis LeDuc

Note(s) to Self . . .

CHAPTER FIVE

THE FAMILY

"Finish each day and be done with it . . .
you have done what you could;
some blunders and absurdities no doubt crept in;
forget them as soon as you can.
Tomorrow is a new day;
you shall begin it well and serenely."

Ralph Waldo Emerson

A few years ago at a family wedding, I started a conversation with one of Jay's cousins. I asked her if she and her husband enjoyed living in Cambridge.

"Yes," she said, "We like Cambridge very much. Our plan was to stay here for ten years and have our children. It has been eight years and we have two children now, so we're getting ready for the next part of our plan. We want to raise the children in Europe."

"Of course," I said.

Well, my husband got an earful that night. "We need a plan!" I exclaimed. "When are we moving to Europe? Blah, blah, blah, shriek, shriek, shriek!" (Did I mention I live in the same city where I was born?)

Run it Like a Business

When my children were small, I went back to school to get my master's degree in business. I was so excited to get out of the house, I actually skipped to class. I usually only took one class each semester but at least I was headed somewhere, learning something new and meeting new people. It reminded me I could do more than change diapers and yell.

In one course, the professor asked us to use our current work experience as a focus to reflect on what we had learned that particular semester. At this point, I had not worked outside the home for several years. Because I was still doing night feedings and was completely exhausted, I was not even embarrassed when I told him I worked at home and the organization I would focus on was my family. He balked at the idea. I said to him, "Look, I may not be selling Pepsi, but I am supplying and shaping the future workforce of America." He was somewhat caught off guard but finally agreed to the topic.

In my paper, I compared managing a family to managing a small business. A family, like a business, must have a budget. Everyday problems, similar to those of a business, would fall under the heading of Operations. And big expenses, like a new car or a kitchen renovation, would come under the Capital Expenditure category. To carry it even further, I claimed saving for a child's education would be the equivalent of a corporation's Research and Development budget. The amount left for savings each year would be the equivalent of profits.

To me, there is nothing more pleasurable than doing business with a well-run organization; things appear to be effortless because they run so smoothly and seamlessly. But it is the painstaking attention to detail, planning, reviewing and reassessing that makes it work this way and seem so easy.

This assignment proved invaluable to me because it enabled me to look at our family within a whole new framework. It helped me to think more clearly and become more focused. I realized it is extremely important to have a family plan with concrete goals and specific steps to get there, not just leave it up to the gods or circumstances. It also became clear how vital it is to weigh all decisions, no matter how small, and to consider the effect those decisions will have on the family as a whole.

Before this revelation, I tended to make individual decisions for each child and not take into account the effect it would have on the family. Recently it was suggested that Emily and Rachel join an AAU (Amateur Athletic Union) basketball team. We had just finished the regular basketball season and I was looking forward to no more basketball for a while. But the talk was, "This is what all the best players are doing. They need to do this to get the edge in high school." Here's that cream-of-the-crop lure again … As I said, it is very hard to ignore talk like this when it is for your children.

Luckily, I happened to be away when all this transpired. My husband reached me on my cell phone to tell me what was going on. He said the games would be every weekend, sometimes both days and sometimes as far as four hours away. Maybe because I was away and not in the middle of all the conversations, the whole idea seemed completely absurd to me. Even a cursory cost/benefit analysis came up lacking. I asked my husband, "Where are we going with this?" I knew my girls would be going to a small high school where the competition was not that fierce, so most likely they would make the high school basketball team. We decided together it would be too big a sacrifice for the whole family to lose all our weekends for 10 weeks, particularly since the girls could achieve their goals without it.

Rachel and Emily did not play AAU basketball that spring. We explained our reasoning to them. We were not dismissing their goal of wanting to play high school basketball; we just felt they could achieve it without putting the family through a grueling AAU schedule. I think they were actually relieved once the decision was made. Kids get tired, too.

The hard part is making the decision, one that works for everyone in the family. In order to do this, it's important to have a plan or vision for your family. Prior to learning to "run it like a business," no plan, no clear goals and no decision-making framework for our family had resulted in a lot of frenzied running around. Don't get me wrong: we still run around. But somehow it seems more directed and purposeful.

Recognizing Roles

In a family, like a business, it is important to recognize each other's role and to realize that they exist. This helped me because, again, it gave me a framework to make decisions for our family. Usually, the clearer I am about what is expected of me, the better job I will do. In a family, one may be a good disciplinarian but not flexible. Another may be flexible but not creative. In a "well-run" family where there is openness, these various strengths can be identified, discussed and dealt with. From this process, each partner tends to take a distinctive role. One handles the money; one decides when the house will be painted; one picks the schools to attend, etc. Not that there are not joint decisions, but usually one person does the ground work for certain areas and makes it happen. Each of these requires different talents and skills.

In my family's particular case, my husband and I had four children very quickly—each a year apart. We decided I would stay home and my husband would work. Because of this, a structure emerged. I was the typical housewife, i.e., taking care of the children, cooking, cleaning, etc. and my husband was the typical "breadwinner" working long hours. We had both worked before the children were born and did not envision ourselves as having the stereotypical 1950's family, but somehow it just seemed to happen.

While staying at home, I realized the role of mother can make you mental. Notice I say "the role" because one summer I witnessed my husband transform before my eyes when he stepped into my shoes for a few days. I was seven months pregnant and our children were three, two and one year old. We went on our one-week "vacation" to Cape Cod loaded down with what seemed like hundreds of playpens, pails and shovels.

On the second day of this vacation, I became quite ill. My husband had to take on my role as "mother." He took care of the children: cooked, changed diapers, cleaned, changed diapers, stopped sand fights, changed diapers, etc. I was so sick that I was bedridden, so I basically assumed the role of the absent working husband. On the fourth day of this delightful situation, my illness started causing complications with my pregnancy. I called the doctor, who wanted me to get to the hospital immediately. I struggled out of bed and went to find my husband. It happened to be dinner time which also happens to be about the same time a husband usually comes home from work and also happens to be the worst time of day for most mothers.

"The doctor wants me to come to the hospital," I said.

"Now?" he screamed.

"Yes," I said calmly.

"Does he have any idea what's going on here? I have three babies I'm trying to feed and bathe!" my husband shouted. "Go back to bed! I'll have to deal with you later!" Right before my eyes my usually calm husband had become the same crazed maniac I am every day at that time. It had only taken three days!

When my husband took on the role of mother, he lost the ability to consider my agenda. He also brought my behavior in the role of mother to the light of day. It made me very uncomfortable to realize this was how I acted many days. I used to rationalize my behavior and tell my husband it wasn't my fault he couldn't see me the seven hours I was good and patient with the kids and would be with him, too, if he were home more. But seeing Jay yelling and out of control like that made my stomach churn. I did not like my husband treating me like that one bit. Is that really how I behaved?

Although it made my stomach churn, I did not change over night. It took time for me to change my behavior because I was pretty deep into feeling justified about my actions. However, my new awareness of my "role" as mother eventually made it quite uncomfortable for me to act like this. I realized more than ever that loving my family is not just an emotion, it is also the way I behave toward them. My behavior shows my love. I learned to stay more in control because deep down I know: I am the adult. My kids watch every move I make. They learn from watching how I treat my husband and how he treats me. If I'm calm and in control, most likely my children are calm and in control as well.

I can't handle all situations well, but I won't handle any of them the way I would like if I am not aware of what I am doing and the effect it has on my family. I say family because I would never think of treating a friend or co-worker the way I sometimes treat my family. It can be very hard being kind to your husband and children, particularly when you feel you are right! So, I keep trying to improve—thought by thought . . . word by word . . . action by action.

My kids are adolescents now and I am finding it more and more difficult not to slip back toward that hysterical person. But I'm more conscious of my behavior and I keep trying!

Family Meetings

Family meetings have started and stopped many times for us over the years. We try to have them a couple of times a month. They stop because the kids may be fighting during the meetings or my husband and I are not in a good place or life is too hectic, but we always come back to them. To relate it back to business, I would compare it to staff meetings. It helps us stay focused and connected and keeps the lines of communication open with our children. At these meetings, our children's differences and individuality seem to become more obvious and we are hoping to notice things in these meetings we might miss elsewhere. We also want to be very sure our kids know and understand our values and, equally as important, know and understand the facts on important issues.

When the kids were young, we would often throw out topics to get a sense of whether or not it was time to talk about certain things. One time my husband asked, "Does anyone know the facts of life?"

"Yes, yes, I do," my son said enthusiastically. "There are five of them, right? The first is education, the second is sportsmanship and the third is religion, but I can't remember the last two."

"That's great," my husband said. "Let's talk about sportsmanship tonight."

Another time when they were young, we decided to have a little lesson on government around an election, so we had them make up "Rules for Congress." This is what they came up with:

- No fighting.
- You should share.
- Listen to your Mom and Dad.
- Clean up when you are done with something.
- Do not hit or kick anybody.
- You will have to be talked to.
- You will be in trouble.
- You will be in deep trouble.
- You will lose your privileges.
- Dad will be really mad.

As the kids became older, the meeting topics have included dating, prayer, problems with friends, sex, vacation ideas, schoolwork expectations, chore issues, mini-maid issues, saving money, and lots of time spent on values and manners. We had them watch a video on the dangers and facts of alcohol and drugs and discussed it afterwards at one meeting.

Though they are less frequent now with two of our four children in high school, we still continue to have family meetings. We all may be busy but we still need to stay focused and connected as a family. And it's more important than ever during adolescence for us to keep the lines of communication open.

Summary

When my children were very young and my husband would come home after work and I was still in my bathrobe (which I swore I would never do), I told him if he ever thought about leaving me for some beautiful, smart, unattached, childless babe—make sure she knew I would be giving full custody of my kids to her and my husband. I dreamed about becoming the hero to my kids every other weekend

To be honest, the thought of Jay with someone else makes me crazy because even on our worst days, I think someone else would be lucky to get him. However, there were many days I felt like . . . *I don't want to do this anymore*. I had never stopped and asked myself—What kind of family life is most fulfilling? I did not stop and think about this for years. I thought I was too busy to stop and think. But actually, I was just completely overwhelmed.

By thinking of my family as a small business, it gave me the framework I needed to make our family life better. Getting organized, stating goals, recognizing roles and engaging in family meetings are some of the ways our family life began to improve. I needed to be willing to change the way we were approaching things and also become more flexible because our family keeps changing. It seems like every few years, as the children get older, we have a totally new family dynamic with new challenges. In order to keep track of all this, I began to write things down in a family journal.

This may sound like a lot of work, but it really was harder for me feeling like I was on a treadmill getting nowhere. I am convinced successful families are not an accident but the result of a tremendous amount of time and focus. Give your family time and trust that time is what it needs.

Steps to Move Forward as a Family . . .

Devise a plan for your family:	Write it down.
Create steps to get there:	Write it down.
Keep track of goals achieved:	Write it down.
Revisit and rethink plan yearly:	Write it down.
Know where you want to end up:	Write it down.

FINAL THOUGHT

"Science has established two facts meaningful
for human welfare:
first,
the foundation of the structure of human personality
is laid down in early childhood;
the second,
the chief engineer in charge of this construction
is the family."

Meyer Francis Nimkoff

Note(s) to Self...

CHAPTER SIX

CHOICES

*"The quality of a person's life
is in direct proportion to their commitment to excellence,
regardless of their chosen field of endeavor."*

Vince Lombardi

Every now and again I begin to feel trapped, as if I have been sentenced to my own life. It usually isn't any one person or thing causing it, but more how I am dealing with my life. I allow myself to be pushed and pulled in lots of different directions by lots of different people. It's as though I am an actor in my own life rather than the director. When I feel this way, I desperately try to remember that life is all about choices. If I have a choice—how can I be trapped?

I had a great professor in college, Ron Billingsley, who ended every class saying, "Remember, you always have choices; you may not like the choices, but remember you have them." This has helped me tremendously over the years. What a fantastic lesson to teach! I don't remember anything else from his class except this one line. It has gotten me through some very dark moments. Life has a way of making us forget we have choices because sometimes those choices aren't great. For me, I need to remember no one is holding a gun to my head forcing me to do whatever it is I am doing. No matter how obligated I feel—it is still a choice. I also need to remember that not making a choice is making a choice as well.

Staying Home

In *Discovering Motherhood,* Robin Morris writes, "I have been thinking about the road less traveled. Since I first heard those words, they have been my ideal. It is not so much because I dislike the beaten path, nor that the unbeaten path holds some great lure. It is because I desperately want to have a life that, in the end at least, *made all the difference*; a life as big and as grand as my personal potential would allow. I did not realize the two roads would diverge at motherhood, although in retrospect it is the most natural place for this to happen to a woman. Yet diverge they did, and choices have been required."

The moment my first child was born, I finally understood the meaning of complete and utter fulfillment. When my husband, son and I were alone for the very first time I knew to the depths of my soul I had been blessed. I fell in love hard and fast and was completely enchanted by the miracle of my son. It was definitely a before and after moment. To this day, I cannot imagine nor have I experienced any reward close to this or one that so clearly defined the path I would choose.

Staying home with my son was not a difficult decision for me. To be honest, I liked what I was doing work wise and seemed to be finding my career path, but I was not passionate about it. Also, I had some complications during my pregnancy and had been put on bed rest which gave me quite a bit of time to think about the life I wanted for my new family.

Initially, I loved staying at home because it was all so new. It gave me time to focus on my son and on myself as a mother. I knew very little about motherhood so I read all sorts of books and articles on the subject. I asked women who I thought were good mothers lots of questions. In some ways, it became my profession because I really wanted to be good at it; isn't that what a "professional" is? When I became pregnant again quite quickly, I pretty much knew I wasn't going anywhere. I was going to be home for a long time.

Although I chose to stay home, this in no way meant all I wanted to be or all that interested me was my husband and children. Nothing could be further from the truth. I did not suddenly lose all interest in the outside world, the desire to talk about other things or the dream to pursue a career. Sometimes, when people found out I stayed at home with my children, their eyes would glaze over. Or they would say something like, "I could never stay home with my kids. My mind would turn to mush and I would be so bored. Aren't you bored?" "Of course, I get bored!" I wanted to say after first strangling them. "But you know what? My kids never seem to get bored with me."

For me, always having interests beyond my family keeps me sane and grounded. I need to be headed somewhere, anywhere that is not facing toward or for my family. I don't know why, but staying at home with children can completely strip you of all self-confidence. A lot may stem from being physically overtired from interrupted sleep. I suspect it also has its roots in the isolation and monotony of the position, as well as the lack of recognition and reward.

As I mentioned earlier, I went back to school part-time to get my master's in business; it took seven years, but I got it! This made me feel more comfortable with my choice to stay home because if something ever happened to Jay, I felt I would be prepared to financially support my family. It also made me feel less dependent on my husband . . . an exit strategy so to speak. I had part-time jobs and took all sorts of classes and attended seminars where I had interests like writing so I could meet new people with similar interests. I wanted to keep developing my skills because I believed it would eventually lead me to where I wanted to be when my children no longer needed me in the same way.

Choosing to Let Go

. . . Of anger

Learning to look at emotions as choices is particularly powerful. For some reason, the concept of *letting go* helped me be able to do this . . .

One day I went shopping with my teenage daughter Emily for a dress for a family wedding. I did not like anything she picked out; she airily dismissed everything I suggested. This was not the fun mother/daughter outing I had imagined. I found myself getting more furious by the moment. Luckily, before I lost it, I was able to stop myself and realize my anger made no sense. I kept my mouth shut and we eventually found a dress that we both loved.

I am learning to recognize that each new phase my children reach brings up new emotions for me, some good and some not so good. The beauty now is I no longer dwell on or become hostage to these feelings. I can actually acknowledge the feeling—like anger—take a deep breath and decide to let it go. I know that sounds a little too simple, but *with practice*, it really works.

I am the one in control of my emotions. I know this is not earth shattering news, but for me it was life changing. Anger is a huge, huge energy drain and I just don't have that much energy. If I do not let go of anger, then I've *chosen* to hold onto it. So if I can decide to hold onto anger, I can choose to let it go.

. . . Of a child

At some point in each of my children's lives I know I will need to be comfortable with the choice to *let go* of them . . .

During college I was going through a particularly difficult time and I was not approachable. One day my father tried *again* to offer me help and guidance of which I wanted no part. By the end of our conversation, he finally said, "We can't seem to reach you. There seems to be so much chaos inside you. This has to be between you and God."

Looking back, he was choosing to *let go* and he was putting his faith in me and God. It meant a lot to me to know he trusted I would find the answers. I hope I have the same courage when it comes to my own children.

Doing Two Things Well

Over the years I learned I can only do two things well at one time. Maybe that's why God only gave us two hands! In trying to juggle marriage, children, career, extended family and friends, I realized at different times in my life I need to make different choices or priorities depending on the circumstances.

Who among us has not tried to do it all and been made miserable in the process? We become completely exhausted from over-extending ourselves, trying to be all things to all people, yet everyone we are trying to please feels shortchanged. The hectic and unending struggle to try and "do it all" has many hidden costs as well: it prevents marriages from growing, kids from enjoying the moment and friends from truly connecting.

For me, being aware of this dynamic helps me make better choices. I ask myself, *what two things at this particular time require my attention?* For example, when my children were babies and I was taking classes for graduate school, I did not have much energy left for my relationship with my husband. We decided to schedule special time for each other on a regular basis.

We hired a babysitter for every other Saturday night for as many months as she would commit. When the babysitter arrived we would head out even if we didn't have specific plans or didn't particularly feel like going out. We also hired Phyllis, who wrote the beautiful Christmas letter at the end of chapter 3, for the alternate weekends on Saturday mornings from 8:30 A.M.-10:30 A.M. and we would go out for breakfast, just the two of us.

Pre-arranging the times to connect definitely helped us during this period. I worried that it was too expensive, but figured it was a necessary investment. The price you pay when you stop communicating is infinitely higher.

During this same time, I had almost no time for my friends. There was not much I could do about it but I still felt guilty and I missed them—I love my friends! So I did what was doable at the time to keep the friendships that were and are so important to me. I started walking early in the morning with friends; I regularly e-mailed to keep in touch; and I made dinner dates three or four months ahead. My friendships—and I—survived.

Knowing I cannot balance all things equally at one time helps me to stay sane. It helps me measure how effectively I am spending my time. This doesn't mean I totally ignore the other important parts of my life. It makes me aware I am neglecting certain things and consequently devise a way to deal with them as best I can given the circumstances. Neglect may be a strong word, but I think this is what can happen if we are not aware of all the pulls on our limited time and energy.

Five-Year Spans

When my son Jim was ten months old, my husband and I had to fly to Chicago (without him) for my younger brother's wedding. We realized we didn't have a will so went to see my brother-in-law who was an attorney. It was a somewhat unsettling but necessary thing to do. Bob drew up our will and as we signed it he suggested we re-visit the will every five years. He said, "In life, you never know what will happen. Don't try to plan or worry more than five years at a time." Less than five years later, Bob died of cancer at the age of forty-two.

I never forgot what he said to us that day. Thinking of life in five-year spans makes life more manageable and choices easier to make. When I chose to stay at home with my son, I thought at the time it would be until he reached kindergarten-five years tops. Well, Jim is now a sophomore in high school and I'm still at home! By the time Jim was in kindergarten, I had three more babies and returning to work was the last thing on my mind. But if, at the time I made the original choice, I thought I was deciding to stay at home for the next fifteen years, I would have been paralyzed by the enormity or seeming foreverness of such a decision.

Life happens. Unplanned events like illness, death, birth, job relocation or financial upheaval occur so new choices are required. None of us knows what the future holds. Making choices within a five-year framework helps me to stay focused on the present. Life changes-choices-aren't forever.

Summary

Life has a way of blowing up in our faces if we are not completely aware of the choices we are making and why we are making these choices. It is easy to forget the quality of our lives is determined by the choices we make every day in every area of our life, including our emotions. By putting my life in a manageable framework, i.e. doing two things well or thinking in five-year spans, I feel more comfortable and confident with my choices. I know and believe in what I am doing and why I am doing it . . . at least for right now.

My oldest will be going off to college in a couple of years. I do not regret for one moment staying home with my children. I am glad I continued to develop my skills because soon it will be time to let go. To be able to do this, I know I will need to be busy with my own life.

My daughter, Emily, who is now fifteen years old and sees so many possibilities before her, recently asked me if I regretted giving up my dreams to stay home with them. "To be honest" I said to her, "You are one of my dreams. And I'm still dreaming!"

FINAL THOUGHT

*"He who cannot change the very fabric of his thought
will never be able to change reality,
and will never, therefore,
make any progress."*

Anwar Sadat

Note(s) to Self...

CHAPTER SEVEN

One time I overheard a woman say, "Sometimes I thank God for my problems because they are attached to the greatest loves of my life." In some ways, this book is a testament to this statement. If you're lucky, your life will be a series of love affairs in all sorts of relationships . . . husband/wife, parent/child, siblings, friends . . . and with relationships come joy, problems and ultimately growth.

St. Exuprey describes love as "the gentle process of being led back to yourself." All of these skills I am acquiring by loving my husband and family are making me a better person. This process is "leading me back to myself." I am becoming the person I always hoped to be.

Sometimes I have to hear something over and over and presented in many different ways until I finally get it. Most of the things I talk about in this book are those things. It's those life lessons we either choose to learn and move on or we choose to stay stuck and miserable. I think it is critical to be totally honest with yourself about what is and isn't working in your life. For me, looking at everything as a skill—like making choices, saying no, thinking long term, forgiving, etc.- has made it more possible for me to change. If I can understand it and I can learn it, I can do it. Solving my own problems actually works.

Perhaps one of the most important lessons I ever learned was that things are not always what they seem . . .

Years ago my parents called me when I was in college 1500 miles away from home. They were each on an extension, so all three of us were talking. I was extremely down and upset as we talked because I was going through a very difficult time. Suddenly my mother said she had to go to the bathroom and she hung up. I remember thinking, "I'm dying here and she couldn't hold it?" I resented her for it tremendously. Toward the end of the conversation my father suggested I come home for the weekend and said he would send me a plane ticket. Once again, my father was the hero. I ended up going home and, to this day, I know it was on that weekend my life started turning around.

A few years later, when I was complaining about my mother to my father he asked me if I remembered the day I called home from college so upset. *Did I remember?* He told me the reason my mother hung up that day was because she ran into the room where my father was on the phone and said to him, "I want her home. Rachel needs to be home." Somehow she knew I wouldn't listen to her. I still marvel at this story because it highlights my ignorance and arrogance and the depth of my mother's love and insight.

I love this story because it illustrates so perfectly that when you are convinced you are seeing things clearly you may not be. And it may take years for you to see things for what they really were. In the early years of my marriage, I was completely convinced my husband worked long hours because he was thoughtless and consumed with his career. I now understand he was overwhelmed, too. Quite quickly he went from supporting himself to being responsible for five more people.

I also love this story because I have faith my own children will have a similar insight. One day Jim, Emily, Rachel and Abigail will realize the depth and magnitude of my love for them, and they will immediately forgive me for all my mistakes.

Before Jay and I were married we had to have a meeting with a priest to discuss why we wanted to get married. When he asked me why I wanted to marry Jay, I said, "He makes me laugh and we have a lot of fun together." This did not seem to satisfy the priest, so he pressed harder, "Are there any other reasons?" And I said, "I'm not kidding; he's really funny!"

Well, eighteen married years later my husband still makes me laugh. I can't think of a better ending to my story.

CONCLUSION

*"Most folks are about as happy
as they make up their minds to be."*

Abe Lincoln

Note(s) to Self...

*think long term, listen,
change what you can control,
say no,
forgive,
plan your life, be willing
to change how you think,
apologize,
laugh,
educate yourself on things
that matter, make conscious
choices, hug,
know you make a difference...*

Printed in the United States
18142LVS00001B/372

9 3 7 3   3